D0607129

THE *FANTASTIC* BOOK OF
Car
RACING

JON KIRKWOOD

COPPER BEECH BOOKS
BROOKFIELD, CONNECTICUT

Designed and
produced by
Aladdin Books Ltd
28 Percy Street
London W1P 0LD

First published in the United States
in 1997 by
Copper Beech Books,
an imprint of
The Millbrook Press
2 Old New Milford Road
Brookfield, Connecticut 06804

Editor
Jon Richards
Design
David West
Children's Book Design
Designer
Flick Killerby
Illustrator
Peter Harper
Picture Research
Brooks Krikler Research

Printed in Belgium

Library of Congress
Cataloging-in-Publication Data

Kirkwood, Jon.
Car racing / by Jon Kirkwood ; illustrated by
Peter Harper.
p. cm. — (The fantastic book of)
Includes index.
Summary: Examines the background and history
of car racing and the construction, operation,
and maintenance of the vehicles used. A detailed
fold-out shows a cross-section of a car, how it
works, and what gives it its speed.
ISBN 0-7613-0581-5 (trade). —
ISBN 0-7613-0565-3 (lib. bdg.).
1. Automobile racing—Juvenile literature.
2. Toy and movable books—Specimens. [1.
Automobile racing. 2. Toy and movable books.]
I. Harper, Peter, ill. II. Series.
GV1029.K486 1997   96-46289
796.72—dc21   CIP AC

CONTENTS

▌NTRODUCTION

For almost a hundred years, the world of motor racing has drawn people with its exciting mix of speed and danger. Since that time cars have been pushed to their limits in an attempt to beat the other competitors on the track. The sport has developed to such an extent that today's racing cars bear little resemblance to their predecessors. Speed is still the key, but the danger has been minimized by strict guidelines and high-tech safety measures.

   Car racing will take the reader around this high-octane world, where hundreds of different types of cars are pitted against each other in competitions of speed, agility, and skill. These include dragsters, rally cars, go-karts, and Le Mans racers. An eight-page fold-out section will show the stages of a Formula One Grand Prix, from preparation and qualifying to the race itself and the winner's podium.

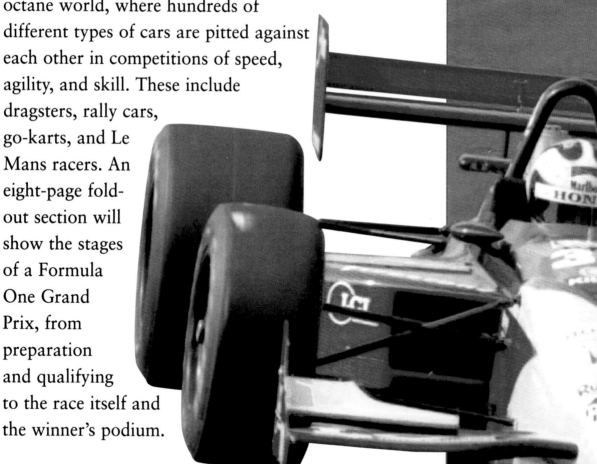

LE MANS RACING

FACT BOX

LE MANS RACER
MCLAREN F1 GTR

LENGTH: 170 IN (4,365 MM)
WIDTH: 71 IN (1,820 MM)
HEIGHT: 42 IN (1,080 MM)
WEIGHT: 2,226 LB
(1,012 KG)
ENGINE TYPE: V-12
ENGINE SIZE:
6,064 CC
(369.9 CU IN)
POWER: 600 BHP
BRAKES: CARBON
DISKS FRONT AND
REAR

Cars that take part in the GT (Grand Tourer) Endurance races need to be lightweight, reliable, incredibly powerful and able to stick to the road like glue.

Perhaps the most famous of all GT Endurance races is the Le Mans 24-hour where cars cover thousands of miles during the course of a night and day. Over the years, some of the greatest names in car-making have entered cars at Le Mans, including Porsche and Jaguar, whose *C-type* models *(above)* won many races in the early 1950s. Today's Le Mans racers, such as the McLaren *F1 GTR* and the Jaguar *XJR (right)* can reach speeds of 200 mph (360 km/h, *below*).

As opposed to the running starts that began the early Le Mans 24-hour race (see page 32), today's race begins with the cars lining up behind a pace car and making their way slowly around the track. When the pace car moves out of the way, the race begins (left). This is called a rolling start.

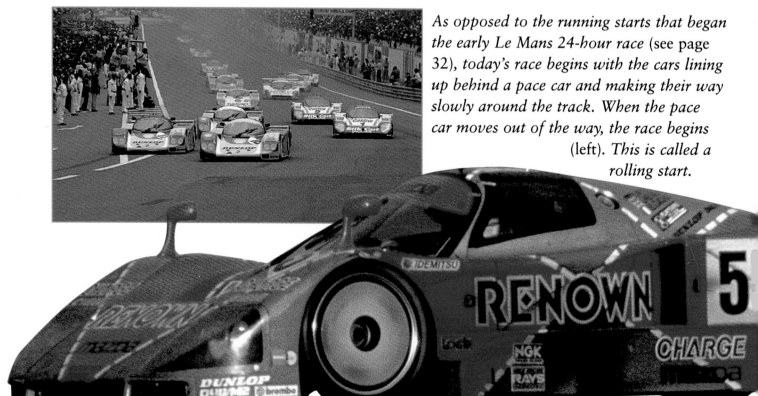

AERODYNAMICS

Racing car designers are forever searching for ways to make their cars sleeker, or more aerodynamic. As it drives along, a car that is not aerodynamic disturbs the smooth flow of wind over it, creating swirls and eddies. These disturbances of the airflow are called turbulence and they increase wind resistance, or drag on the car which slows it down. A racing car is designed to cut through the air without creating too much turbulence, letting the air flow smoothly over it. Such a car is described as aerodynamic.

Racing cars make use of the airflow to generate downward force. Wings attached to the racing car act like upside-down versions of an aircraft's wings, creating downward force instead of lift. This downward force presses the car tires onto the track so they get better grip, allowing the racing car to go around corners faster and brake harder.

1

2

Some racing cars use air ducts at the front of the car 1 *(above) to generate more downward force. In the McLaren F1 GTR (above) there are fans* 2 *which suck air from underneath. As a result, pressure beneath the car is reduced, increasing the effect of the downward force.*

A Formula One car has wings on the front of its nose and a further wing on its rear to create downward force (below). These wings can be adjusted before a race to alter the amount of downward force needed. The downward force generated at 188 mph (300 km/h) is enough to stick the car to the ceiling!

Aerodynamic shape ensures car cuts through the air easily

Rear fins create downward force

Smooth flow of air under the car

Rear wing

Front wings on a Formula One car

Air-flow

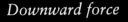

Downward force

DRAG RACING

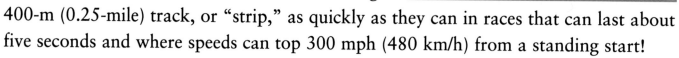

Drag racing is a flat-out challenge of speed and acceleration. Cars hurl themselves down a straight 400-m (0.25-mile) track, or "strip," as quickly as they can in races that can last about five seconds and where speeds can top 300 mph (480 km/h) from a standing start!

A wide range of cars race at drag meetings, from the needlelike Top Fuel dragsters (main picture) to stock cars and the so-called Funny Cars. Despite this variety, all the models will have been stripped down to the bare essentials and fitted with amazingly powerful engines in an attempt to shave vital hundredths of a second off the time for each race.

FACT BOX

A TOP FUEL DRAGSTER

LENGTH: 300 IN (7,622 MM)
WIDTH: 56 IN (1,420 MM)
HEIGHT: 90 IN (2,290 MM)
WEIGHT: 2,100 LB
   (955 KG)
ENGINE TYPE: EIGHT
   CYLINDERS WITH
   SUPERCHARGER
ENGINE SIZE: 8,000 CC
   (488 CU IN)
POWER: 6,500 BHP
BRAKES: HAND-LEVER
   ACTIVATED CARBON FIBER
   DISKS, FRONT AND REAR
   A PARACHUTE

At the start of a race,
dragsters spin their wheels
to improve tire grip.
This is called burnout.

FUEL

Normal gasoline is not powerful enough to drive dragster engines. Instead, they use a variety of different fuels. The fastest cars, the Top Fuel dragsters, burn a nitromethane mixture. Other cars use a mixture of alcohol and methane that does not deliver as much power but is a lot cheaper to use. In a single five second burst, a dragster engine can guzzle up to 15 gallons (57 liters) of fuel. With all this flammable liquid around, mishaps can occur *(below)*.

A turbocharger (below) is a device containing a turbine 1 *turned by exhaust gases* 2 *from the engine. The turbine drives a blower* 3 *that compresses air and blows it into the engine increasing the pressure of the fuel/air mix* 4 *, boosting power, and improving fuel efficiency.*

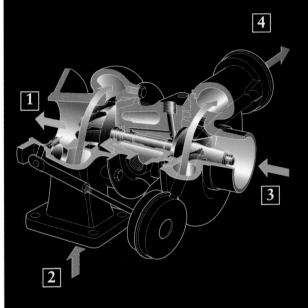

BOOSTING THE POWER

Turbochargers and superchargers are ways of greatly boosting an engine's power. For example, since turbos were banned from the sport in the late 1980s, a typical Formula One engine can only produce 700 bhp – before they were banned a turbo-charged engine could produce 1,200 bhp!

Because turbochargers only work when the engine reaches a certain point, the surge in power they deliver is delayed. Cars, such as dragsters, needing an immediate surge in engine power use superchargers. In these, the turbine is driven directly by the engine and not the exhaust gases. This boosts the power as soon as the engine is started.

GO-KART RACING

The small size of the vehicles used makes kart racing an ideal place for the young driver to start in car racing. Indeed, over half of today's Grand Prix drivers began competition behind the wheel of a kart. The small costs involved in karting make it one of the most popular forms of motor racing to take part in. Literally hundreds of different classes exist, determined by engine size, fuel type, driver's age, weight of the car and driver, etc... It all adds up to an exhilarating sport where speeds can reach 160 mph (260 km/h)!

1

*Disk
brakes*

2

*Brake
pads*

When the brakes of a car are applied they heat up due to friction between the brake pad and the wheel. In a racing car, they can glow red hot (right).

BRAKING AND SUSPENSION

Disk brakes 1 (*left*), where pads are squeezed against a disk that rotates with the wheel, are the most effective form of braking system. Because the disk can lose heat easily to the air it is less prone to "fading" – where brakes become less effective because of the pad or shoe heating up. Drum brakes, where the brake "shoes" are forced against the inside of a brake drum 2, are less effective because they cannot lose heat as easily as disk brakes, making them more likely to "fade."

Car suspension has to deal with the bumps in the track, keeping the wheels in contact with it. Most car suspension has a spring 1 and a piston 2 inside an oil-filled cylinder 3 (*right*). Together, they compress and extend to absorb any bumps. Racing car suspension (*above*) is stiffened, so that the car does not rock too much and can corner as quickly as possible.

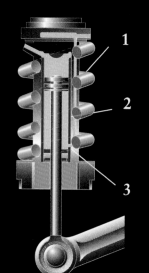

1

2

3

KARTING

Karts are raced with a minimum of bodywork – little attention is paid to the aerodynamic requirements of this vehicle. The most a kart might have are a bumper on the front and rear and two panels, one on either side. The engine sits behind or to one side of the driver. In the sport's early days, these engines were taken from old lawnmowers.

GETTING A GRIP

In dry weather (or indoors!) racing cars have slick tires $\boxed{1}$ (*below*), with no tread pattern, to get maximum grip. In the rain, however, cars change to special wet-weather tires $\boxed{2}$. These have a deep tread cut in them which is designed to disperse water and keep as much rubber in touch with the track as possible. Off-road tires $\boxed{3}$ also have a deep tread to get the maximum grip while driving over rough terrain.

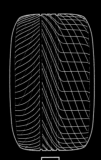

$\boxed{1}$

$\boxed{2}$

$\boxed{3}$

Kart circuit

Kart racing is fast and furious, with cars usually bunched closely together as they hurtle around circuits that can be up to 0.6 mile (1 km) long (left). Because the performance of the karts in a class is pretty much the same, it is usually driver skill and daring that gets a kart to the front of the pack.

RALLY-CAR RACING

Driving beyond the comforts of a tarmacked race track, rallying is not a sport for the faint-hearted. Rally cars fly along private roads, dirt tracks, or across country, sometimes within a hair's breadth of trees or a sheer drop. Accidents are frequent (left), but the cars are fitted with tough safety cages and harnesses to ensure the safety of those inside.

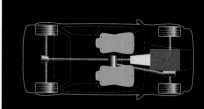

1 In a four-wheel drive car all four wheels receive power from the engine, which is often at the front of the car. However, some four-wheel drive cars have mid-mounted engines.

Although they look similar to production cars, rally cars differ greatly from road-going machines. They have been specially prepared for the tough races. Engines are tuned and semi-automatic gears (see below) are fitted. Many rally cars also use four-wheel drive because this offers them the maximum grip when driving over conditions that can range from gravel to mud and even through water!

Off-road rally car

GEARS

A gearbox is a casing containing cogged wheels, called gears 1 (above). These change the ratio of revolutions between input 2 and output 3 shafts, allowing the car to drive at different speeds. Many racing cars are also fitted with a semi-automatic gearbox. Instead of moving a cumbersome and time-consuming gear stick, the driver merely flicks a switch to change gear.

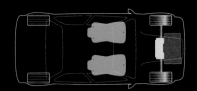

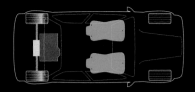

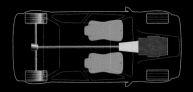

2 *A front-engined, front-wheel drive car is the most common orientation in modern, road-going cars. Front-mounted engines tend to make cars more stable.*

3 *In a rear-engined car, an engine behind the driver drives the rear wheels. This configuration is common in high-performance cars, including Grand Prix cars.*

4 *Most road-going cars have an engine at the front driving the rear wheels. Putting the power on in a corner in a rear-wheel drive car tends to make the car oversteer.*

Rallying and off-road racing can take a hefty toll on a vehicle. After each stage the cars are stripped down (below) and serviced to ensure they deliver maximum performance for the next part of the race.

FACT BOX

RALLY CAR
SUBARU IMPREZA 555

LENGTH: 171 IN
   (4,340 MM)
WIDTH: 67 IN (1,690 MM)
HEIGHT: 55 IN (1,390 MM)
WEIGHT: 2,640 LB
   (1,200 KG)
ENGINE TYPE: FUEL-
   INJECTED, FOUR-CYLINDER
   WITH TURBOCHARGER
ENGINE SIZE: 1,994 CC
   (122 CU IN)
POWER: 300 BHP
BRAKES: VENTILATED DISKS
   AND FOUR-POT CALIPERS

FORMULA ONE RACING

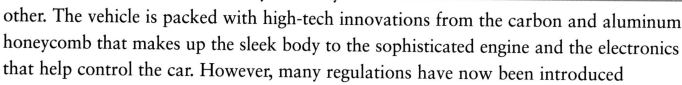

The shape of today's Formula One racing car owes more to the aircraft industry than any other. The vehicle is packed with high-tech innovations from the carbon and aluminum honeycomb that makes up the sleek body to the sophisticated engine and the electronics that help control the car. However, many regulations have now been introduced restricting the use of electronics.

The car is even equipped with a small black box recorder, similar to those used in all modern aircraft. This records all of the actions of the driver as well as the data about the car. This can be used to spot what caused an accident.

Since the early days of car racing, the shape of Formula One cars has changed beyond recognition. Even in the 1950s, cars such as the Mercedes W196 (above) still had *front-mounted engines. Today's rear-engined cars, such as the Ligier driven by Oliver Panis (below),* are designed for a combination of speed, agility, and safety.

FACT BOX
FORMULA ONE CAR FERRARI 310
LENGTH: 171.5 IN (4,355 MM)
WIDTH: 78.7 IN (2,000 MM)
HEIGHT: 37.4 IN (950 MM)
WEIGHT: 1,310 LB (595 KG) WITH WATER, OIL, AND DRIVER
ENGINE TYPE: V-10
ENGINE SIZE: 2,998 CC (183 CU IN)
POWER: 700 BHP
BRAKES: CARBON DISKS AND PADS FRONT AND REAR

F1 COCKPIT

The driver of a Formula One car is squeezed into a very tight cockpit *(right)*. In front of him there is an array of instruments that helps to control the car and keeps him informed about his performance. These instruments include warning lights that tell him when to change gear, an indicator of which gear the car is in, and a selection of readouts that can include lap time and speed. There are controls to adjust the fuel-air mix in the engine's cylinders and to fine-tune the strength of the brakes.

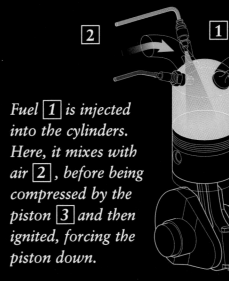

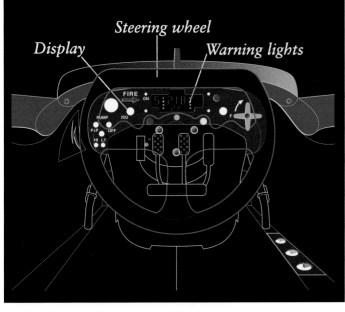

Display

Steering wheel

Warning lights

Fuel 1 *is injected into the cylinders. Here, it mixes with air* 2 *, before being compressed by the piston* 3 *and then ignited, forcing the piston down.*

FUEL INJECTION

Many racing cars have electronically controlled fuel-injected engines *(above)*. Fuel injection gives accurate control of the fuel-air mixture in the cylinder. A computer figures out how much fuel is needed and when it should be injected into the engine's cylinders. It does this by measuring a number of factors when deciding how much and when to inject fuel. These include the level of engine revolutions per minute, the position of the throttle, and the pressure of the air in the inlet system.

The computer is programmable both before and even during the race so that the demands for more power (a richer mixture) can be balanced against fuel economy (a diluted mixture) at all times.

Headphones in the driver's helmet relay instructions from the pit lane to the driver. At the same time, the car sends information through a radio link back to the pits where engineers can check its performance.

DRIVER'S PROTECTION

In the early days of racing competitors would drive wearing ordinary clothes. If there was an accident – especially a fire – there was no real protection for them. Today, however, drivers are covered from head to toe in clothing designed to keep them safe in the extreme heat and danger of a fire. Topping off the outfit is a lightweight, but extremely tough crash helmet.

HEAD PROTECTION

Modern helmets weigh only 2.6 lb (1.2 kg) and have padded linings under the hard exterior. Some helmets are aerodynamically shaped to encourage air flow into the engine air inlet which is right behind the driver's head. Beneath the helmet, the driver's head is covered with a fire-resistant balaclava (*above*).

UNDER THE OVERALLS
A full set of fire-resistant underwear (left) *is compulsory when you get into a Grand Prix car. The long-sleeved top and full-length underpants are complemented by socks and the balaclava. Some drivers wear up to four layers of this protective clothing, leaving only the eyes uncovered.*

Grand Prix

Teams will arrive at a circuit from the Wednesday before the race. In the period before race day on Sunday the pit area is busy as teams prepare the cars. Everything needed for the race has to be readily available. This includes: 1 spare body parts and wings; 2 engines – up to ten engines may be used by each team; 3 spare wheels. Also required are computers, compressors and, of course, tools.

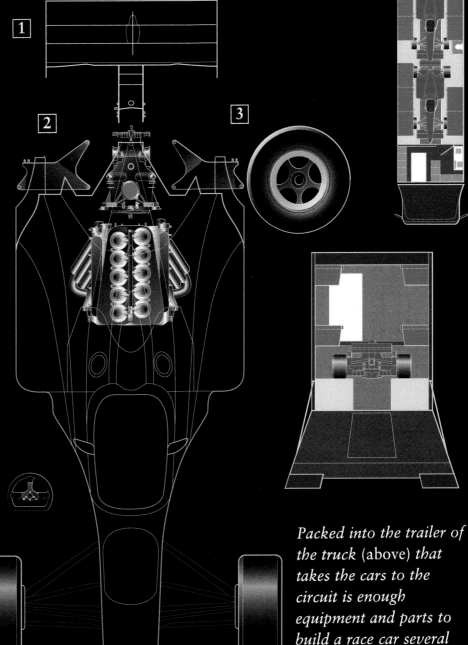

Today's Formula One teams carry about 25 tons of cars and equipment to each race in massive, specially built container trucks (below).

Packed into the trailer of the truck (above) that takes the cars to the circuit is enough equipment and parts to build a race car several times over. Trailers have an upper storage area that the cars are lifted up to by a tail lift. They are also equipped with an air-conditioned office that has a telephone and a fax machine. This can be used for technical debriefings during the time at the circuit.

Qualifying

On the day before the race, drivers have two practice sessions where they can test the performance of their cars. The Saturday afternoon before the race is the qualifying period. For one hour only, drivers have 12 laps to record their fastest lap. This time will decide their position on the grid – the quickest driver will start in pole position *(below right)*.

Throughout this qualifying period, the cars are equipped with special engines tuned for qualifying and they run with fuel tanks that are very nearly empty to keep the weight down and the speed up.

End of race

Danger

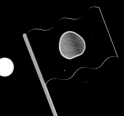

Mechanical problem

All clear

The race has been stopped

Pole position

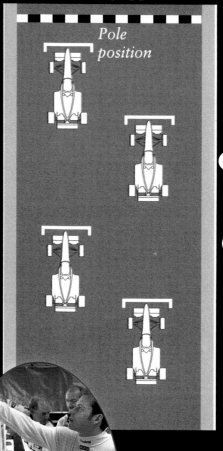

Before, during, and after qualifying, the teams will scrutinize masses of information about both the car and the driver's performance (above and right). This information will include technical data about the car, such as fuel consumption, power output, lap times, and a video of how the driver performed around the track – all of this in an effort to improve performance and grab that vital pole position.

Pole position (above) is at the front of the grid, offering the driver the best approach to the first corner. Behind this the cars are staggered, with two cars on each row.

The Race Officials

There are a number of flags used by officials to let drivers know about race conditions *(left)*, such as a slippery surface, or to give them instructions and information, including warning them of unsportsmanlike behavior. The one every driver wants to see is the checkered flag.

Unsportsmanlike behavior

Slippery track

One of the duties of the officials is checking the driver's performance *(below)* and the car after the race *(above)* to make sure that they have conformed to the rules. Among other things, they will check that the correct type of fuel has been used and also examine a device attached to the underside of the car. This device is used to stop the cars riding below the minimum legal height for the base of the car, which is 0.3 in (10 mm).

Designated car must stop at pits next time

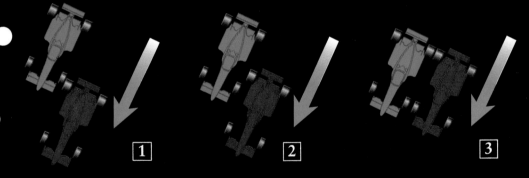

1   2   3

A driver is looking to overtake

In a collision, the blame depends upon the situation. In [1] (above), *it is the fault of the blue car because he has not gotten far enough up on the car in front and cannot claim the racing line. In* [2] *,the responsibility is shared because both cars have equal claim to the racing line. In* [3] *, the red car is at fault because the blue car has gained enough ground to claim the racing line.*

Slow vehicle on track

BEYOND FORMULA ONE

Outside the world of Formula One, safety plays just as important a role. Dragsters, saloon cars, rally cars, and stock cars are fitted with a safety cage that surrounds the driver. Dragsters are also fitted with an in-car fire extinguisher system that sprays both the engine and the cockpit. They also have an escape hatch in the roof.

At positions around the circuit, marshals are stationed where they can wave flags to warn drivers and assist in an emergency. There are also specially equipped fire marshals (right) who can respond to a fire within seconds. Cranes may also be available to lift a damaged car clear of the track (above).

SAFETY IN RACING

Safety is of paramount importance to all concerned in car racing. This is not just the safety of the drivers, but also of the spectators, race officials, and team members.

Technological advances have led to the fitting of black box recorders to racing cars *(see page 14)*. Super-strong materials are now used to make a racing car's body, forming a protective shield around the driver. Other, more simple ideas have also been introduced. These include the use of gravel traps that can slow cars quickly and tire walls that can absorb much of the force of an impact.

HARNESSED

Drivers have a full six-point safety harness to keep them securely restrained in the cockpit. Like other safety features and equipment, the harness must be approved by the FIA, the official body of motor racing. There is a quick release in the center of the harness so the driver can get out of the car quickly when it stops. Some racing cars are also fitted with a removable steering wheel (*right*) that can be easily pulled out in the event of a crash to let the driver escape quickly.

Pace cars (below) are brought onto the track in most forms of racing if an accident occurs. The remaining cars must line up behind this slow-moving vehicle until the problem has been cleared. The pace car then moves out of the way and the race begins again.

To warn drivers about the presence of a slow or official vehicle on the track, the marshals wave white flags. If the accident is very severe the race may be stopped altogether.

ROLL BARS

In many forms of car racing, drivers are protected by a roll bar (*left*). This can be as simple as a single hoop of steel that sits just behind the driver's head. Should the car flip over, this simple yet strong device stops the driver from being squashed.

The roll bar in a Formula One car is built into the bodywork in an unobtrusive manner, sitting around the engine air intake. Along with the tough carbon fiber casing that surrounds the driver, this makes the cockpit of a Formula One car virtually indestructible.

THE WORLD'S CIRCUITS

Most race circuits in the world – apart from the oval tracks used in Indy racing – are a combination of straights, where the cars accelerate up to their top speed, and different types of bends. The circuits are designed to give cars and drivers an all-around test so that top speed is not the most important factor. Handling around the bends can become just as important. Different types of bends call for different techniques from the drivers.

Most circuits are in areas where there is plenty of space, but there are also some circuits in towns and cities, such as the Monaco Grand Prix *(see page 31)*.

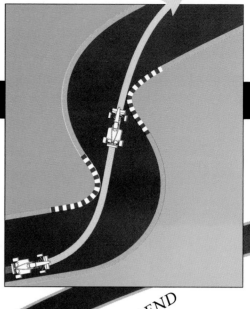

S-BEND

S-BEND
At an S-bend a driver brakes before turning into the first of the two bends. He then accelerates through and out of the second bend (above).

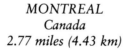

MONTREAL
Canada
2.77 miles (4.43 km)

CHICANE

START/FINISH LINE

PIT LANE

CHICANE
The chicane is a series of tight turns in opposite directions in an otherwise straight stretch of a track. To stay as fast as possible drivers have to keep braking to a minimum amount and try to "straighten out" the bend by picking the best racing line (right).

SILVERSTONE
GREAT BRITAIN
3.266 miles (5.226 km)

HOCKENHEIM
GERMANY
4.25 miles (6.802 km)

SPA-FRANCORCHAMPS
BELGIUM
4.34 miles (6.94 km)

MAGNY-COURS
FRANCE
2.669 miles (4.271 km)

MONZA
ITALY
3.625 miles (5.8 km)

ESTORIL
PORTUGAL
2.72 miles (4.35 km)

SUZUKA
JAPAN
3.665 miles (5.864 km)

HAIRPIN

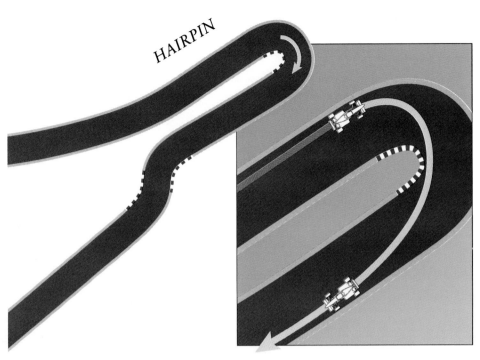

HAIRPIN

A hairpin is a U-shaped turn in a track where the cars turn by 180 degrees (above). Drivers have to brake hard and then turn late. As they move around the bend they accelerate before straightening.

THE PITS

In the pits of any race the mechanics play a vital role in keeping the car on the track. In a Formula One race the pit crew can be huge (about 20), but in Indy racing the permitted pit crew is just two mechanics (*below*). All the mechanics wear protective overalls, made from Nomex, the same material used to protect the drivers (see page 16).

To ensure safety in the pits, Formula One drivers must keep their speed below 75 mph (120 km/h). Anyone breaking this rule faces strict penalties.

Modified road-going cars are used in stock-car racing *(left)*. However, major alterations have to be made to them. These will include fitting safety cages, a race-tuned engine, racing seats, and driver harnesses. Car-to-car contact is common and cars will often nudge each other, especially when cornering, to gain an advantage.

AROUND THE BEND

There are many different kinds of lap-style car races – from the all-out oval-circuit racing of the Indy races to the tortuous town races in cities such as Monaco. Some of the fiercest racing takes place using cars that are recognizable as cars you might be able to buy and run on the street. And some only slightly modified vehicles engage in a crash-filled spectacle of stock-car racing that can result in very few finishers, such as the NASCAR series *(right)*.

OVAL CIRCUITS
In banked oval circuits, cars do not have to slow down as much for corners as they do on nonbanked circuits. This is because the banking counteracts some of the forces created by the car turning. To give them further help around the banked corners, Indy drivers can raise one side of their car using compressed air.

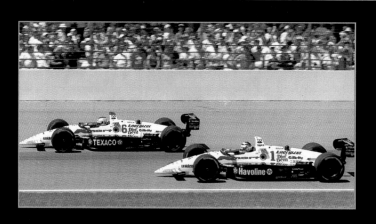

CITY-BASED RACES

Racing around a city, as with the Grand Prix de Monaco *(right)*, has its thrills and special problems for the driver. It is very hard, for example, to overtake when races are held in narrow streets. At such a race, getting pole position is very important. There are other hazards with city-based races. Should the driver come off the track, there is no run-off area and the car will hit a wall or a barrier instead of coming to a stop on gravel or grass.

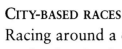

The National Association for Stock Car Racing (NASCAR) holds races for stock cars around oval tracks. These cars regularly record lap speeds in excess of 200 mph (322 km/h).

INDY RACING

In Indy racing, cars hurtle at high speed around oval circuits *(right)*. The test is of speed, stability, and nerve. The cars are not that different from Formula One. The sport is named after the Indianapolis Motor Speedway at Speedway, near Indianapolis, Indiana. The 2.5-mile (4-km) track, nicknamed the "Brickyard," is the oldest racing track still in use. It is the venue for the Indianapolis 500.

GOING THE DISTANCE

With endurance races, the emphasis isn't so much on speed, as it is on actually completing the race, keeping both driver and machine going until the finish. These races include the nonstop 24-hour races such as Le Mans and the rallies that can cover huge distances in separate stages over roads, tracks, or across country.

At the end of every Monte Carlo Rally competitors have to race in a hill-climb section where they are timed on a course through the surrounding hills (below).

Early Le Mans races would start with the drivers sprinting across the track to their cars (left). However, this has since been replaced by a rolling start (see page 6).

RALLY NAVIGATION
Seemingly alone in the middle of nowhere, a car on a long-distance rally raises a cloud of dust as it navigates between checkpoints *(left)*.

Getting lost is one of the major hazards of long-distance rallying and the role of the navigator is made doubly important as time is precious. A wrong turn can cost vital seconds, minutes, hours, or even days!

Perhaps the most famous of all rallies is the Monte Carlo Rally (below). Since it began in 1911, hundreds of competitors have started from different points throughout Europe and North Africa heading for the Mediterranean resort of Monte Carlo. Weather conditions have always proved a key factor in this winter rally. So much so, that in the 1965 race, only 22 cars out of 237 finished the race.

RALLYING

Rallying has a long history and began way back in 1907 with a race between Peking and Paris. It took competitors over 60 days to cover a distance of 7,500 miles (12,000 km). The East African Safari, which was first run in 1953, is the longest rally that is held regularly: It covers an incredible 3,874 miles (6,234 km).

RACING ODDBALLS

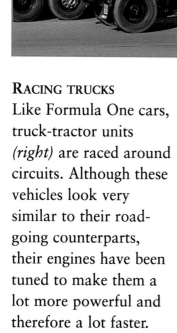

People will go to amazing lengths to alter their vehicles. In this case (above) a truck has been fitted with counterweights to let it pull "wheelies." Some trucks have even been fitted with jet engines. One, called Shockwave, can reach 376 mph (605 km/h).

If it has wheels and a motor, the chances are that someone has raced it. Everything from production cars straight off the street to special models made for hill climbing, giant trucks, tractor units of freight vehicles, and veteran three-wheelers have been or are a part of the race scene – some people will even race lawn mowers!

RACING TRUCKS
Like Formula One cars, truck-tractor units (right) are raced around circuits. Although these vehicles look very similar to their road-going counterparts, their engines have been tuned to make them a lot more powerful and therefore a lot faster.

MONSTER TRUCKS AND RACING TRACTORS

Some of the most extraordinary machines used in "races" are found in dirt-filled arenas. So-called Drag Tractors bear little resemblance to the farming vehicles (*left*). In a trial of strength, these powerful tractors try to pull increasingly heavier loads over a set distance. Monster trucks (*below*) are basically normal trucks fitted with huge wheels, enormous suspension, and a powerful engine. These vehicles are raced around dirt tracks, leaping over obstacles and crushing cars.

A SMASHING TIME

Some "races" are little more than trials by combat where cars deliberately smash into each other on a mud or dirt track until there is only one left that can actually continue moving. This car is declared the "winner." The cars used for these races are prepared to make them safe for the driver, with harnesses and safety cages. However, not much effort is spent making the bodywork look attractive (*right*).

RACING HISTORY

Almost as soon as cars became practical, they were being raced. Racing satisfies not only the competitive instincts but it is a means whereby car manufacturers can test out new technology. Over the years, this desire for competition has led to the development of many different forms of racing all over the world.

By pushing engines and other components to their limits, car makers have learned how to make cars not only faster but also more economical, more efficient, and more reliable. So racing has been of great importance in furthering the development of automobiles generally.

The first Grand Prix race was held in France in 1906 at Le Mans, France (above). *The winning driver was Ferenc Szisz* (below) *driving a Renault. He led a field that included 34 cars, 25 of them French and nine being German and Italian. The race was held on two succesive days and involved six laps of an enormous 64-mile (103-km) circuit.*

LE MANS: THE BENTLEY YEARS
One of the dominating forces at Le Mans during the 1920s was the British Bentley team. Since the first 24-hour race in 1923 until the close of the decade, Bentleys won five of the races, losing in 1925 and 1926 to the Lorraine Dietrich team. The picture *(above)* shows a Bentley in the 1930 race, a race that was to be their last success at the historic meeting.

RACING IN AMERICA

The first car races that took place in the United States were the Vanderbilt Cup races. Launched in 1904, the races were held over a triangular course on Long Island, the first being won by American George Heath driving a Panhard.

Since that time, the number and type of races has multiplied. Perhaps the most famous in the United States being the Indianapolis 500 (so called because the race was over 500 miles). The first of these races was held on May 30,

1911, when American Ray Harroun won driving a Marmon Wasp. The picture *(above)* shows an alarming incident from the 1932 race, when Billy Arnold crashed. Other races included the Santa Monica Grand Prix, which had the famous "Death Curve." Here *(left)* Johnny Marquis crashes during the 1914 race.

The changing appearance of racing cars can be seen in this "parade" (below), ranging from the Sunbeam Tourist to the McLaren Ford.

1914 Sunbeam Tourist

1950 Alpha Romeo 158

1954 Mercedes W196

Chaparral 2E

1969 Matra

1973 McLaren-Ford

DURING THE WARS

Most forms of car racing were postponed during the two World Wars. Instead of producing more racing cars, many factories and workshops were turned over to producing munitions *(left)*. Grand Prix racing began in 1921 after World War I and in 1947 after World War II.

LOSSARY

Aerodynamics
The science of how objects move through the air. In car racing, an aerodynamic car is one that slips through the air, creating little turbulence, or drag.

Airfoil
In car racing, a wing that provides downforce as the car moves through the air.

Axle
This can be a shaft on which a wheel revolves, a revolving shaft with a wheel on it, or a rod connecting two wheels.

Bore
The diameter of a cylinder in an engine.

Burnout
In drag racing, the spinning of tires while the vehicle is stationary before a race to get them to the temperature where they give the most grip.

Calliper
A braking component in which friction plates press against a rotating disk.

Capacity
The size of the engine. It is the amount of air that is displaced by the engine's cylinders during a single cycle.

Chassis
The supporting framework of a car. In many racing cars it is a frame made from metal tubes.

Cockpit
The space for the driver, controls, and instruments.

Connecting rod
The connecting or "con" rod links the piston to the crankshaft in an engine.

Cylinder
A hollow chamber found in engines in which a piston slides back and forth.

Downforce
A force created by the wings or bodywork of a car as it moves through the air. It pushes down on the car, improving its roadholding ability.

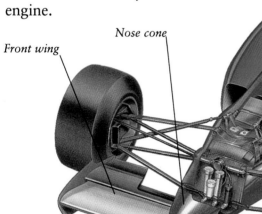

Front wing

Nose cone

Rear wing

V-10 engine

Rear disk brakes

Safety harness

Front disk brakes

FORMULA ONE CAR

Drag
A force acting on a car as it moves through the air. It is caused by turbulence in the car's airflow and slows its progress.

Engine
The device that turns energy into force or motion. An internal combustion engine, such as a gasoline or diesel engine, converts energy released by burning of the fuel inside its cylinders into motion.

Fade
The tendency of brakes to become less efficient after repeated use because of heating of the braking surfaces.

Fuel injection
This gives accurate control of the fuel-air mixture in the cylinder. In many cars, a computer calculates how much fuel is needed and when it should be injected for optimum performance.

Gearbox
The casing containing gears which change the ratio of revolutions between input and output shafts.

Pole position
The number one position at the front of a racing grid.

Roll cage
The framework built into a car to protect the driver in the event of a crash.

Shock absorber
A device that absorbs sudden shocks to the suspension of the vehicle.

Slick
A tire with no tread, and usually made of a soft compound for maximum grip.

Suspension
A system of devices – usually springs, linkages, and shock absorbers – that supports the upper part of a vehicle on its axles.

Transmission
A system of shafts and gearboxes that transmits power from the engine to the axle of the vehicle.

Turbine
A device comprising a shaft fitted with blades that is turned by the flow of a liquid such as water or a gas such as steam through it.

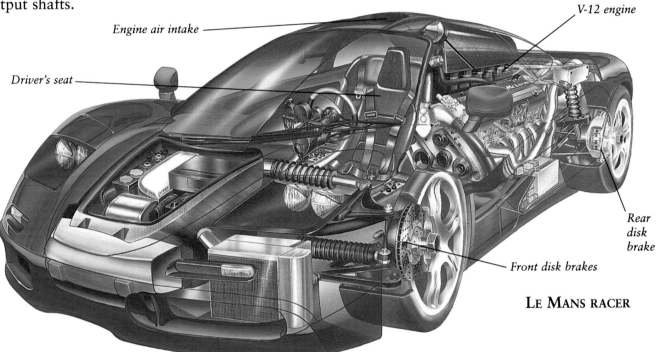

Engine air intake

Driver's seat

V-12 engine

Rear disk brake

Front disk brakes

LE MANS RACER

Methanol
A type of alcohol that is used as a fuel in certain racing cars.

Nitromethane
Also known as "nitro," a fuel component that gives enhanced performance.

Piston
A disk or cylinder that fits tightly within a cylinder and moves back and forth.

Stroke
The distance a piston travels up and down in a cylinder.

Supercharger
A device that blows air into the engine inlet to boost its power. It contains a fan driven by mechanical linkage from an engine.

Turbocharger
A device containing a fan that is driven by a turbine by exhaust gases from the engine. The turbocharger blows air into the engine, raising the pressure of the fuel-air mixture in the cylinders, boosting the engine's power output.

Wheelbase
The distance between the front and rear axles of a vehicle.

Index

Photo Credits:

Abbreviations: t-top, m-middle, b-bottom, r-right, l-left
Front cover – Honda UK. 3, 4-5, 10 both, 11 both, 14m, 14-15, 15t, 16 all, 17, 18m & b,
23b, 24m, 25t, m & b far r, 26mr & b, 27 all, 29 both, 30b, 31tl & b & 33t – Empics.
6t & b, 7b, 8-9, 19, 20m & b, 24t & bl & 26t – Rex Features. 6m, 14t, 20t, 20-21, 21t,
mt, mb & bl & 23t – Zooom Photographic. 6-7, 12tl, 12-13, 13b, 18t, 21br, 22 all,
25bmr, 26ml, 28, 31tr, 32b, 35 all & back cover – Frank Spooner Pictures. 7t – Mercedes
Benz Foto. 8t & 9 all – Neil Smith. 13m & 30t – Ford UK. 24br, 25br, 34 both & 34-35
– Eye Ubiquitous. 25b far r, bl & bm, 32m, 32-33t, 36 all, 36-37 & 37b – Hulton Getty
Collection. 25bml & 32-33b – Solution Pictures. 30-31 – British Film Institute.
37t – Mary Evans Picture Library.